ESPRESSO VOL. 2

ORLANDO KIMBER

The Arthur & Moose
Publishing Company

CONTENTS

PREFACE

'Wisdom is the principal thing; therefore get wisdom.'
Proverbs

In ancient Greece, the idea of 'a good life' was one built on affection for others, making a contribution, and having the poise to think carefully; qualities within the reach of anyone. If you were to believe in the message of today's media, the definition of success is a commodity to push, the celebrity to get column inches, and lots of money. This is not a criticism of fame or wealth, but it is a questioning of our values. What kind of world do we want to live in, and how can we create that world? This is the realm of ethics.

The word 'essay' comes from the old French word for 'trial'. Michel de Montaigne, Benjamin Franklin, Samuel Johnson and George Orwell all used this form to explore ethics through events and ideas that fascinated them. Like these giants of thought, many of us are interested in discovering a feeling of truth about what lies behind the current changes in all aspects of society, the environment and economy.

To do this, I've brought together facts, reasoning and principles of secular ethics to explore both the public ideals and the reality that each of us now face as a global citizen.

Orlando Kimber, December 2021

SELF

TRANSITIONS

When a painting student suggested his work was in 'transition', his tutor said that was OK, as the reverse (of the word itself) is 'no it isn art.'

All of us, whether creating, managing a business or simply growing older, must pass through transitions. Although each will be different, they share common underlying features.

The first phase is the end of an old order in which we experience a breakdown, even collapse, of familiar patterns, relationships and processes. What used to work no longer functions in the same way, and this can be very confusing.

The next phase is that of emptiness, where there appear to be no signs, guideposts, familiar territory or landmarks. Many then panic, and either cling to whatever they had before – no matter how dysfunctional, painful or profitless it may be – or grab whatever they can for 'security'.

While one can feel isolated and bewildered at this stage, there's a purpose to it which will only become clear later on, when small indications and possibilities half-suggest themselves.

Gradually, as one gets a sense of distance from the original state, one feels a growing confidence and understanding that there is an underlying shape and meaning to the change. Without the barrenness of the stage that precedes this, one wouldn't even notice these new ideas.

Finally, there is the undeniable, solid and evident feeling of arrival at the other side of the transition, and the beginning of a different way of doing things.

The key to it all is to keep smiling!

HOPE

After love, hope is surely one of the most valuable human emotions. Times of struggle bring the significance of hope, with its forward-looking nature and unequivocal qualities, to light.

Viktor Frankl, in his remarkable little book *Man's Search for Meaning*, details the importance of hope in enduring three years as a prisoner of war during World War II. The ideas that sustained him and others were an intense feeling of love in a personal sense and the determination that, should they survive, they'd ensure such an atrocity would never happen again. It was this driving purpose and conscious intent that enabled them to bear the hardships and brutality of everyday life in the camps.

No doubt this would not have been possible without a care for fellow humans of future generations. They certainly longed to be with their loved ones once again. Perhaps the terrible crimes meted out against prisoners incited further righteous anger and outrage in their hearts. Hope gave their tribulations meaning. Every cruelty, every privation, and the myriad examples of inhumanity the prisoners had to witness were fuel for their purpose. Frankl believed this was the sole reason that survivors lived to tell the tale. Our individual freedom of thought and independent liberty of action is just as essential to us in modern times, even if we're not marshalled by cruelty or penned in with barbed wire.

VENGEANCE

That it's commonplace for humans to seek revenge is all too obvious. Whether this is in the heat of an alleged blind fury, or served cold as a deliberate act, may have some bearing on a legal decision. Either way, the intent is to hurt someone who (you believe) has harmed you.

This payment of aggression with aggression results in a continuous loss on both sides, until one party withdraws from the conflict. We see it in every kind of human relationship, because we're programmed to act like this. We were told 'an eye for an eye' in the Old Testament. Doesn't it feel right when the bully gets their due? This idea of reciprocation becomes downright perverse when humans take their rage out on loved ones, or inanimate objects, when they don't respond as expected.

There is a way out of this. Things don't have to escalate to an all-out war, and it only takes one side to figure this out and act on it consistently. Gandhi (a Hindu) didn't agree with much about Christianity, but he revered the words of Jesus in the New Testament: 'If a person should strike you on the cheek, offer him the other.' This accords with the principle of Ahimsa, or non-violence and respect for all living things. Eastern philosophies hold that violence inevitably has harmful consequences, and that good outcomes for our lives come from decent actions in the present moment. This is the essence of karma.

However, it is necessary to stand up to oppression and, by definition, this requires the courage to face a bully. We do not differ from one another. We all long for happiness and each has natural human weaknesses, including ignorance. It is well to remember this, whether we decide to pocket an insult to keep the peace, or respond to a hurt with firm, coherent words that make our case.

Happily, others came before us to show the way.

FORGIVENESS

The story of the prophet Jonah and the Whale is common to Christianity, Islam and Judaism. Its origin is the Bible, which tells the story of the son of Amitai (literally meaning 'truth'). God sends Jonah on a mission to tell the town of Nineveh that they will pay a price for their sins. As a mere human, he thinks the task looks too difficult and flees in the opposite direction. He's travelling by ship at sea when a fierce storm blows up and Jonah confesses to those on board that he is to blame. The sailors then dump him overboard and the sea immediately becomes calm. The delighted crew prepare a sacrifice to God, while Jonah is swallowed by 'a giant fish'. He seems doomed to die there.

The next part of the story tells of Jonah praying, begging forgiveness, and committing to being grateful for his life and following a righteous path. At this, God commands the fish to vomit out the penitent Jonah, so he can complete his mission.

The prophet duly arrives in Nineveh, predicting calamity in forty days. Within just twenty-four hours, he's convinced the entire population (including the king) to admit their wickedness and humble themselves in sackcloth and ashes.

Yet when God then saves the town from destruction, Jonah is unhappy that they are to go unpunished for their sins! This leads us to the ultimate moral of the story as 'Forgiveness comes to everyone who deeply regrets their wrongdoing, not just yourself, who you judge is worthy.'

GAMBIT

A contestant may sacrifice a piece, typically a pawn, early in a game of chess. This is a gambit – literally a 'tripping' manoeuvre – in which the loss of the material allows some kind of gain to the player. An opponent may avoid taking the piece offered for sacrifice, because they understand that they'll ultimately suffer a greater loss; taking the piece may disrupt their own strategy by putting their own material out of position. Alternatively, the player offering the sacrifice may wish to open a corridor for a certain attack. Finally, there's the possibility that the initiator gains some kind of first-mover advantage to help them dominate the game. When a computer considers the same options, it uses error-free calculating, machine learning, searches (from a library of perhaps 30 million moves) and programming, to work out how to use the current circumstance to its advantage. Evidence-based judgement is helpful in decision-making.

In the seventeenth century, the mathematician and philosopher Blaise Pascal used logic to produce one of the earliest examples of game theory. He simply said what Christian, Islamic and Sanskrit writings had suggested before, that 'God either does, or does not exist. Given that we have to choose, it's wiser to believe in God, as the benefit of getting it right in our life far outweighs the minor loss of some physical pleasures that we may sacrifice.'

However, while Pascal rigorously applied the principles of reason, he accepted that in this case, he was surveying infinity.

CARE

Many people use the word 'care' (from the twelfth-century English *cearu*) correctly, in the sense of being burdened or worried or anxious. The other usage of 'to care for someone' has a different root. This sense of the word is closer to the Latin *caritas*, which in the Bible is interchangeable with 'to love', hence 'And now abideth faith, hope and love' (Geneva version, 1560).

This combines the idea of giving one's attention to someone or something, and to help without expecting or getting anything in return. It's very similar to the Buddhist and Baha'i notions of loving-kindness, a term that also appears in sixteenth-century translations of the Bible.

Care suggests both kindness in action and taking advantage of an opportunity to reinforce a link with others. The motivation to do this may spring spontaneously from putting oneself in another's shoes. If we permit ourselves to witness someone's genuine suffering, we naturally compare their situation with our own. When we experience the difference between one situation and another, a compelling desire to take action arises spontaneously. Many flee before this point, as the feeling of altruism can disperse as soon as it arrives unless we take action.

It's said that doctors who put all their attention on curing patients are condemning themselves to a life of frustration: recovery, especially among the frail, is never certain. Those who dedicate themselves to caring for rather than curing patients have limitless potential for success.

◉

RELAX, JUST RELAX

There's a passage in the book *Autobiography of a Yogi* by Paramahansa Yogananda, in which he describes sleep as an opportunity for a human to experience the total freedom of a soul unfettered from the body. He points out that when we dream, our movements are no longer defined by practical considerations of effort or space or time, but merely by our mind. If we think something, it becomes, albeit in our imagination.

Yogananda practised Kriya Yoga, with the object of strength and health without a high level of physical exertion. This is certainly not the case with all styles of yoga.

Using the mind to produce an unseen effect also pertains to the practice of Qi Gong (pronounced chi gung), a set of ancient Chinese exercises designed to optimize physical vitality. The discipline here is to practise gentle exercises and to sense the feeling of energy (the *chi*) that flows in our body.

We might define fitness as a constant supply of energy that enables us to do what needs to be done, regardless of age or disposition. Modern cultures highlight aerobic workouts to build this capacity, and these certainly benefit the body. However, while activity and movement are common to all systems, Qi Gong and Yoga emphasize liberation from emotional turmoil as a key element in maintaining health. They define vitality by the strength of the immune system and general well-being rather than muscle size and tone, and consequently place the use of imagination above that of willpower.

Excessive stress is now commonly recognized as harmful. Whether you go east or west, you will find no practice that advocates skipping sleep to build mental or physical strength, unless specifically replaced by meditation or prayer.

ADAPTIVE LISTENING

The ability to listen effectively depends on the reliable functioning of the physical auditory system (the ears and brain), concentration and the relationship of a sound source to our location. Although we only possess two ears, our hearing is omni-directional, presumably to help us sense quarry or predators in our ancient hunter-gatherer days. If we hear a noise louder through one ear than another, our brains perceive the source to be closer to that side and thus we form a stereo image.

We can find a dramatic demonstration of this in modern binaural recordings. The earliest of these had the sound of a matchbox shaken first on the left, then the right, and then round the back of the head and over the top. Definitely 3D. I urge you to try it with headphones, and marvel at your own ability to decipher sounds and derive meaning from them.

Our brains are so smart that in the environment

of a noisy cocktail party, we can filter out extraneous sounds and focus on the conversation we're having. In such an environment, the sound field of the room is composed of many voices, rich in frequencies at differing volumes. Fortunately, research has proven that if we alter the position of our head in relation to a sound source we're interested in, the brain has to recalibrate against the target it's pursuing. This results in a temporary loss of intelligibility and may account for why we don't catch someone's name. A poor excuse, but a scientific one.

THE EMPEROR AND THE DRONE

Dwellings normally afford their inhabitants private rooms, whether it be a salon or bedroom. In ancient China, architects arranged palaces in concentric squares, which allowed public access only to the outer rooms. The further one penetrated the building, the more personal the living space. Even if Google Earth had been available two thousand years ago, the emperor would still be safe from prying eyes.

In this digital age, when online access is universal in the industrial world, we have not defined privacy as a right. The technology to monitor citizens globally continues to multiply in both strength and reach and we know that national security services constantly ingest our calls, email and web activity. Given that both the state and businesses have access to the traces of our online life, the police (for instance) simply need a warrant to get access to the records.

Your personal life is therefore vulnerable should anyone have the motive and means to attack. Computer worms or hackers can infiltrate a system and offer content to third parties, so as far as intellectual property goes, the only way to secure one's digital data is to keep it on a discrete device that's never linked to the internet.

We can see a more visceral development of this in the micro-replicas of the remote-control craft, as used by the US in Afghanistan and Pakistan to attack military targets. These extraordinary nano-drones are proliferating worldwide and now have a DIY culture. How will owners use such devices and, with miniaturization allowing ever smaller components, what can we then do to maintain our physical privacy?

CULTURE

A HARDSCRABBLE LIFE

Martha Jane Cannary was born in 1852 in Missouri, St Louis; the oldest of six. At fourteen-years-old, she and her family travelled over 1,400 miles by wagon to Salt Lake City, Utah. When she lost her mother to pneumonia on the trail, Martha had to step into her shoes and run the family.

Just one year on, her father also died, and young Martha packed her siblings back into the wagon and took them 400 miles north-east to Wyoming. She had learned to shoot well and ride fearlessly, but she remained illiterate and worked on and off at whatever jobs she could get, including prostitution.

In Martha's autobiography of 1896, she tells the story of how she gained fame after rescuing an officer single-handedly during a military campaign against native American Indians. This account conflicts with one by the adventurer John 'Captain Jack' Crawford, who recalled her as 'notorious, dissolute and devilish, but possessing a generous streak which made her popular'. She became known as 'Calamity Jane, Heroine of the Plains'.

By her forties, she'd lost her youthful charms and was working as an army scout. It was then that she claimed to have married Wild Bill Hickok and later, to have pursued his murderer with a meat cleaver, having left her guns at home. It certainly seems that her offence was to 'court calamity', but it was also said of her that, 'Her vices were the wide apart sins of a wide open country – the sort that never carried a hurt.'

DRUMMING

As soon as humankind could breathe, walk and feel a heartbeat, drumming was present.

Some of the earliest instruments found are slit drums – a gash gouged out of a tree trunk – and there's evidence of ancient stones arranged to form a primitive xylophone. It can't have been long before early humans discovered that empty shells, or even the mouth of a cave, would amplify sound. From this concept there sprang hollowed logs with a skin stretched taut on top, beaten by hand or sticks. In Indonesia, the gamelan evolved into an entire orchestra of drums, metal keys, gongs and resonators, played in complex sequences and rhythms.

Drumming is common to all cultures worldwide and stems from simple two, three or four beat modules, put together in limitless variations. The most sophisticated example of this is in Indian classical music and dance, which even has a language to narrate the complex patterns known as *tala* or *taal*. These rhythmic structures can be anything between three and 108 beats, and yet allow for great freedom of expression.

Over the ages, we've used drumming for signals, ceremony, celebration, dance, war, healing and prayer. Shamans the world over drummed to induce trances in themselves and others as an essential part of their rituals. Rhythm ranges from simple monotonous thumps, to a continuous cascade of beats that trigger an irresistible response in the animal part of the human psyche. That pulse is in us all.

◉

MOVING STONES

Rings of standing stones created thousands of years ago around Britain and France remain a testament to the reverence and truths of the Neolithic age.

Stonehenge, set high on a plain among Wiltshire's rolling green hills; Carnac stretching long fingers of stone out towards the Atlantic on the coast of Brittany; Callanish standing proud in the wilderness of Lewis in the islands of the Outer Hebrides; and countless other ancient temples scattered in between, far and wide, great and small.

Whenever I visited such prehistoric sites as a child, it wasn't just the wonder of these enormous edifices, inhabiting remote places, that struck me. It was also the fact that they'd remained in place. Sure, sometimes landowners have moved individual stones to hasten the building of a new cottage. Perhaps a few farmers have also sought to obscure works and thus avoid contamination of their land with tourists, but in many cases these structures remain as enduring as the timeless landscapes they stand in.

Their context is as important as the structure itself. Professor Alexander Thom proved direct correspondences between the alignment of stones and the heavens. He concluded that whoever had constructed the stone circles (not giants, as was believed in the Middle Ages!), had sited them according to precise astronomical observations. He was thus able to confirm specific sites as either lunar or solar calendars. In a time when science was apparently so crude, it's astonishing to consider that these vast edifices conform to such subtle and accurate measurements. The result is an architecture that's withstood the test of time, both literally and aesthetically.

POESY

For the last four thousand years, we've used written language to communicate both everyday events and the meaning we give to them. Just as ordinary thoughts may seem of less interest and urgency than grand passions, so poesy (literally 'creation') has always been our vessel for moments of heightened emotion or importance.

The earliest surviving fragments of poetry are from Mesopotamia (now Iraq) dating back to the second millennium BCE. These include clay tablets inscribed with the epic of the giant king, Gilgamesh. The Chinese *Book of Odes*, composed a thousand years later, includes both sacred and secular works. This is one of the Five Classics of Confucian philosophy, in which the authors addressed both the correct regulation of society and yet also saw fit to include love songs. The immortal Indian sage Vyasa (Krishna) wrote the *Mahabharata* five hundred years after this, with two hundred thousand lines of verse. Like the *Book of Odes*, its origin is likely to be songs and oral epics.

The oldest surviving epic in British literature, *Beowulf*, relates:

Sea-weary still, they set their broad,
Battle-hardened shields in rows

to create a profound and beautiful poetic expression. A sense of perfect and convincing truth is the mark of great literature.

While we use plain prose for laws and reasoned debate, the role of poetry has always been to move audiences in ways that logic would not. Unfortunately, populist politicians use this same technique to poison rather than clarify debate. As Seneca said, 'Whenever the speech is corrupted, so is the mind.'

OVER THE HILLS AND FAR AWAY

The six-volume, last edition of *Wit and Mirth: or, Pills to Purge Melancholy*, was published in 1720. It included over a thousand 'witty ballads, jovial songs, and merry catches', one of which was featured in *The Beggar's Opera* written by John Gay just eight years later. 'Over the Hills and Far Away' was an uncharacteristically sweet duet between a lover and his lass. The lines alternate between the two characters:

> And I would love you all the Day,
> Every Night would kiss and play,
> If with me you'd fondly stray,
> Over the Hills and far away.

The irony of this is that Gay's work lampooned the upper classes by portraying the lead characters of his opera as thieves and whores. Inspired by the success of *Gulliver's Travels*, Gay determined to write a biting satire on the foibles of the rich in

England, such as their professed love of Italian opera. He pointed the plot at the political and moral corruption in society; particularly the ability of the wealthy to purchase justice and the social inequality that led to the squalid living conditions of the poor.

The great revival of satire during the Enlightenment esteemed wit, rationality and clear thinking. No treasured principle or institution was safe, including Members of Parliament and the church.

Despite the threat of legal action, the power of satire remains available to us today. It may be that we're always in need of fresh, thoughtful, articulate, amusing and very public challenges to sacred cows.

SCHRÖDINGER'S CAT

Early twentieth-century physicists discovered phenomena at a subatomic level, which didn't conform to classical theorems that worked so well to describe macro-level stuff in the material world. It therefore forced scientists to develop alternative propositions that reliably described these new incidents accurately and repeatedly. These proved to be counter-intuitive.

To illustrate this, the Nobel Prize-winning physicist Schrödinger offered a fictional demonstration: a researcher puts a cat into a sealed box, with a flask of a lethal substance. The toxin may (or may not) contaminate the box during the cat's confinement, thus threatening its life. According to the models of quantum physics, the cat is simultaneously both alive and dead while in the box. In classical thinking, it's obviously one or the other, as any observer can confirm.

Schrödinger was not satirizing the theories of quantum physics. He was asking, 'At what point does one stop applying the common-sense assumptions of reality and instead apply the correct alternative thinking?' Albert Einstein praised Schrödinger for the rarity of his honest appreciation of the issue.

Perhaps there's a parallel here that we can all easily comprehend. We vaunt logic as the great thinking tool of our scientific age, yet there's a domain in our lives which appears to operate according to different rules: the entanglement of relationships and love. While we struggle to understand the everyday tangible events of our outer world by applying classical thinking of 'reason', could there be an altogether different and more appropriate procedure used by our hearts and minds?

ZHAO MENGFU

Before Kublai Khan's Mongol hordes conquered all of China in 1279, the final resistance came from the Sung people. Zhao Mengfu was a civil servant and a descendant of a Sung emperor, yet he took office under the invaders and rose to become a provincial governor. His outstanding talent, however, was as a painter and calligrapher and he later regretted his decision to serve those who had overthrown his family.

Many artists of this period withdrew under foreign rule and the new dynasty did not encourage native Chinese culture. Despite this, and perhaps because of his compliance with the regime, Zhao Mengfu became renowned for a new style of painting. He rejected the refined and gentle technique of the previous period for cruder brush strokes. He often layered the middle ground to increase a feeling of depth in his works and excelled in depicting natural objects. With Zhao, landscape painting reached a further climax of development in China.

Among his influences were the great ninth-century artist Dong Yuan and the eighth-century painter and poet Wang Wei, whose 'poems hold a painting within them'. Many of these survive today. Ultimately, Zhao developed a cool, detached sense of understatement in a revival of a 'spirit of antiquity' which had followed the arrival of Buddhism in China a thousand years before. Ironically, Zhao's move towards simplicity afforded him a direct, unaffected personal expression, so at odds with the loss of political power among the Sung.

UNDERCOVER HEROES AND HEROINES

Most of us go through life attempting to conceal our traits, flaws and weaknesses in the belief that this makes us more socially acceptable. While this is superficially true, it can also make it harder to sustain relationships.

When a secret agent goes undercover, the hazards of working against dangerous foes are obvious. Additionally, their assumed identity can cause tremendous stress, as it can cause a schism with their actual character and personality. The challenges of integration back into their previous lifestyle can also be complex.

Knowing this makes the work of the British Special Operations Executive (SOE) formed in 1940 – shortly after the start of World War II – the more remarkable. They recruited male and female agents from all backgrounds to spy, sabotage and reconnoitre across Europe and to support the growth of resistance forces. For this, they needed a deep knowledge of the country (particularly the language), diplomatic and 'rough soldiering' skills.

Two of the most renowned SOE agents were Violette Szabo, operating in France, and Patrick Leigh Fermor who lived in the Cretan mountains for two years. Violette was the daughter of a London cabby and joined the SOE at just twenty years old, on the death of her husband. Known as 'Louise', she took part in two missions, the second leading to her capture and death in Ravensbrück concentration camp. Fermor survived to become a respected author. Ninety-one men and thirteen women of the SOE died in action.

◉

THE FIRST CORNISH REBELLION

The year was 1497, and to pay for his punishing war on the Scots, King Henry VII raised taxes across England. In Cornwall, the most southwesterly region of the land, a statute dating back to 1201 exempted the local assembly (the Cornish Stannary Parliament) from paying national taxes. Henry's counsellors suspended the law and threatened closure of the assembly unless the Cornish yielded a thousand pounds – about six million in today's money – to the crown.

A lawyer named Thomas Flamank declared the tax illegal and stated that he would take a petition of the people's grievances to the King. Fatefully, he also said that he would name the evil counsellors in person.

Flamank, together with Michael An Gof, a blacksmith, summoned a force of 15,000 men armed with billhooks, bows and arrows, for an orderly march of two hundred and sixty miles to London. They modestly declared that they would command the army 'until more eminent men were found' and gathered influential support from all levels of society. However, the march had disheartened and exhausted the militia by the time they arrived on the outskirts of the capital. Many fled, and the King's forces defeated the remainder at the Battle of Blackheath.

The King ignored the Cornish petition, and both Flamank and An Gof met the gruesome death of traitors; hanged, drawn and quartered at Tyburn gallows. The King released many of their followers, but Flamank had these words of warning that echo through the centuries down to the present day, 'Speak the truth and only then can you be free of your chains.'

WORK

INCLUSIVITY

Truly democratic organizations are 'inclusive', as opposed to those which are ruled by elites which are termed 'extractive'. Inclusivity, therefore, is the policy of not excluding or favouring anyone because of gender, race, class, sexuality, disability or religion. It demands treatment on individual merit rather than by category. This makes excellent sense for any business on several levels, not least because it requires employees to dispense with the bias of their own opinions; the same conceit that will also skew their ability to think clearly about practical problems.

The capacity to assess circumstances and to make a judgement – particularly regarding those with whom we associate – is a vital tool for leadership and anyone who aspires to it. Preconceptions, unless built from actual knowledge and experience applied to the current circumstances, make fools out of us all. It's as if we'd rather cling to a fallacy we're familiar with, than be attentive to what's actually happening right now in front of us.

For a consumer-facing business, including all people regardless of external differences simply reflects the diversity of their market. Buyers will value this if they also receive the service they expect. There's also a subtle message for the employees of an inclusive company, which is one of respect. Isn't this simply the golden rule of 'do as you would be done by' in action?

PILASTER

A pilaster is the term for something that looks like a pillar but is, in fact, an ornament. They can be supportive, but normally they merely stand there looking elegant in relief against a wall. They are the lounge lizards of architecture that do nothing other than look nice.

Maybe there are equivalents in all fields? Perhaps in politics, one might look at certain government ministers and say, 'I understand we may need one of those, but I'm not sure exactly what it is they do.' In business, too, there are figures who flit in and out of the office, but whose purpose is notoriously hard to pin down. They may be glamorous agency 'PR girls' who drop in for important meetings, i.e. when they're pitching, never to be seen again. Come to think of it, there are entire industry segments that seem pointless but must have a purpose. Otherwise, they wouldn't be there, would they? Consultants, for instance. If the board won't allow the CEO of a business to decide on a strategy or policy without consultants, what are they there for?

The noble full-supporting column can be graceful too, as anyone visiting the Acropolis can testify. However, I leave it to you to discern whether the international bailout of Greece in 2011 provided necessary structural strength to the local economy. It required €110 billion (albeit with a 50 per cent write-off by creditors a few months later), a further €130 bn debt in 2012, and some smaller contributions 'to meet debt repayments up to 2019'. The total is at least €295 bn, and the schedule for repayments extends beyond 2060.

It looks like the Eurozone may have created pilasters of its own, as it is the ordinary citizens of Greece who must bear this debt that 'supports' them.

SAFETY AT WORK

Across Europe there are well-publicized health and safety guidelines for both office and manual workers: employers must not only protect their staff but also involve them in the identification of hazards. During 2017/8 in the UK alone, employers lost about 30.7 million working days from work-related illness (26.8 m) and workplace injuries (3.9 m).

For manual workers, the challenges come from machinery, operations (such as repetitive strain injuries) and the environment. For office workers, the physical threats are as likely to be a burn from a scalding mug of soup. However, the greatest risk to all workers appears to be how to manage the demands on their time, and the consequent levels of stress and fatigue.

Medical residents and mine workers alike may work eight consecutive twelve-hour days. Although the physiological effect may be modest, studies have shown this will impair their judgement. Significantly. A survey by the American industrial safety pioneer Herbert Heinrich (1886–1962) estimated that unsafe acts caused at least 80 per cent of workplace incidents. Like the father of modern quality management, William Deming (1900–1993), he believed correct training for team members to enable them to do a job responsibly is important, but not the only factor. Both Heinrich and Deming concluded that safety depends on the entire culture of a company.

Therefore, to measure the quality of a company's management, you need look no further than their commitment to optimum health and safety. Though it may seem irrelevant to commercial performance, it is evidence of their ability to think and behave correctly.

CERTAINTY AND RISK

Common sense tells us that if we throw a six-sided dice there's a one-in-six chance of a three coming up so, logically, the likelihood of a three occurring in six throws of the dice is 100 per cent. Wrong, because the events are independent. I won't go into the maths here, but trust me on this ...

Because humans are fallible, economists have adopted models of game theory which apply mathematics to conflict and cooperation between rational decision-makers. Such calculations work well when each party is motivated solely by the same outcome in a transaction, such as a cash reward. However, they are not so useful when one side seeks a different benefit from the other, has different degrees of intelligence or suffers 'irrational' feelings.

The potential of a loss arising from a chosen action is 'the risk', originally a term specific to the insurance of cargoes traded across seas. From this commercial root sprang the analysis of possible scenarios, ranging from the worst to the best. We're seldom (if ever) in a situation where we have perfect knowledge with total security from error, so it's normal for us to make decisions with a partial view of the facts. Furthermore, we may have good quality information, but we cannot know what the future will bring, other than a change in the context of the original decision.

Politicians and business persons trading with other people's money are not always aware of, or clear about, the degree of certainty and risk in a situation. For this reason Warren Buffet observes that it's 'always best for players to have skin in the game ...'

PROMISES, PROMISES

Corporate banking as an industry has been party to terrible disruption in economies around the world. It might therefore be instructive to examine the history of investment banking and financial services, through the prism of one of the largest multinational firms.

Marcus Goldman founded Goldman Sachs in 1869 and began by trading promissory notes (aka commercial papers) to entrepreneurs. These documents promise to pay a stated sum to a named individual, on a specific date or on demand. Their success, therefore, depends on funds being available when they're required. When one such fund failed in the stock market crash of 1929, the economist J. K. Galbraith later noted of this case and others that it 'was, perhaps, the first occasion when men succeeded on a large scale in swindling themselves'.

From 1930 onwards, Goldman shifted towards

investment banking and developed a culture which both restored confidence in the bank's ability to raise capital, and to provide advisory services. However, by the 1950s and under the influence of a new partner, it returned to trading notes. Goldman subsequently took the helm and in 1970 a further financial crisis threatened the firm. Once again, Goldman Sachs swung back to more sober investment practices that boosted their reputation.

In 1976, the senior partners confirmed fourteen pragmatic business principles that, at the time of writing, the company's website still displays. The first of these refers specifically to putting a client's interests first. Integrity to this principle is a hallmark of all good business, as long as the client's requirements don't conflict with wider ethical values such as environmental or social harm.

In recent years, and looking more widely across the industry, it's become universally apparent that powerful organizations need to work within an objective monitoring system rather than be trusted to self-regulate. As a caveat, J. K. Galbraith declared that, 'The sense of responsibility in the financial community for the community as a whole is not small. It is nearly nil.' The violent economic eruptions of history echo this point, and the consequences are no longer local. They are global.

OFFICE POLITICS

All of us suffer tests and occasional failures and there's no disgrace in that. They challenge us to get up after a fall, brush ourselves down and set off again in our eager quest. This is tough if there's an atmosphere of pessimism or other negativity pervading our home or workplace.

The best environment for enthusiastic, happy and productive people, is one that cherishes these attributes. How often are these characteristics the determining factor in a work-related interview? It's rare to see a job description which lists the ability to 'work in harmony with others' for a role. When a company requires outstanding abilities, it's normal for them to select a candidate for their technical skills or knowledge. Yet if the employee is antisocial, the team will disintegrate despite the individual's qualifications of assumed excellence as a functional unit.

There are also those who like to craft an illusion of their importance, by excluding others from access to valuable information. This is extremely damaging to trust and morale and, as the miscreant may be skilled in covering their tracks, hard to address. When such behaviour is endemic in an institution, there is only one conclusion: it's condoned by the management, either openly or by neglect.

However, there are companies which insist on employing contented people, because they recognize these souls want to see the organization thrive and will thus share information appropriately. Smart managers know that untroubled staff celebrate the success of their peers whereas unhappy people like to disrupt the status quo.

None of this is news, but it deserves to be reiterated. We survive and thrive by the cooperation and trust of others in all the domains of our lives.

CAMPAIGNING FOR ELECTION

Besides the critically important question of the suitability of a candidate for a public post, they must wage a campaign to convince voters of their worth. Over 90 per cent of those nominated for elected office in the UK represent a political party. This suggests a benefit to being allied with a well-known faction, and the huge advantage of both funds and votes attracted by such an association.

When a young man or woman's fancy turns towards politics, the challenge of how to finance a successful campaign will immediately demand an answer. While the goodwill attached to a cause will vary with conditions, hard cash is important. How else is one to activate the wide array of communication tools, such as events and social media advertising, that are so useful for drawing attention and delivering a message? While sound policies, practical goals and realistic plans are vital to encourage the voters' faith in an inspiring leader, nothing works better than face-to-face encounters to establish rapport and spur action to vote. Digital is convenient, but digits on the end of a hand are better. Real-life meetings are also the best way of finding out what constituents actually need. Clever two-dimensional ideas formed on paper must be tested in the three-dimensional world. Often, they are not.

The eternal dynamic of time, quality and cost persist. You can campaign with good quality and at low cost, but should not expect to achieve this without plenty of time.

TEMPO, TEMPO

'Allegro con moto' is not Italian for 'travelling fast with the roof down in a Ferrari along an autostrada', but perhaps it should be. I'd like to tell you we never used the term before Mr Benz patented his first racing car, but alas, the composer Luigi Boccherini predates him by about a hundred years. The origin of the musical term 'con moto' goes back to before the internal combustion engine and means 'with motion'. Therefore, 'allegro con moto' means to perform a musical piece quickly with motion or urgency. However, since the white heat of industrial revolution propelled us into an age of high-speed travel, composers have written more musical works with this instruction.

Happily, there are many other tempi, qualifying terms, instructions and moods in music, which naturally reflect the various rates at which we lead our lives. For instance, in our working lives, there are those who take their affairs at what we might call 'larghetto' (rather broadly), and these have typically been in the public sector. Technology businesses tend to run at the other end of the range from 'vivace' (lively and fast) to 'prestissimo' (the fastest). The latter normally ends in an uncomfortable adjustment when the wheels come off. There is no musical equivalent to this.

The best-run companies – consistently profitable, with steady growth, a happy environment and high standards – seem to hold a constant 'allegro moderato' (moderately fast, but only just above medium pace) with occasional bursts of 'vivace'. Perhaps it's because this is a manageable velocity for groups of mere humans to sustain ... What tempo is your working environment?

DINOSAURS

Monstrous and fantastic beasts dominated the globe for 135 million years until an extinction event snuffed them out 65 million years ago. Their remains were first recognized in the early nineteenth century, and have been objects of persistent public enthusiasm, media attention and scientific research ever since.

Likewise, the early nineteenth century saw the marketing of prehistoric oil deposits as 'barrels', standardized in 1860 at 42 gallons. Fuel companies now supply enough to fill about fifteen Empire State Buildings a day, or 93 million barrels in old money.

Consumption comes at a cost: both financially (which an eagerly growing industrial society seems happy to pay), and in terms of pollution through the production, transport and usage of hydrocarbons. This includes environmental damage in Ecuador, Nigeria, Columbia, Azerbaijan and Kazakhstan, and disastrous marine oil spillages such as that of the *Exxon Valdez* (Alaska, 1989). Since 2010, there have been more than seventy incidents. Their total spillage would fill one Empire State Building; twenty-seven times the volume of the *Exxon Valdez*. Add to this the consideration of emissions from burning fuel both in production and use. Finally, there are instances such as the Iraq and Falkland conflicts, where oil was a crucial factor in a state's willingness to go to war, with a terrible social impact.

In the twenty-first century we know so much more about the consequences of our addiction to hydrocarbons, yet we appear to have moved no further than regulating the storage and transport of oil distillates ... and allowing governments to reap the tax from their sale.

This presents international oil and gas companies with a huge dilemma between respecting our perishable environment on one hand and enjoying the short term rewards on the other. Will Big Oil and Gas wait for an extinction event to snuff us all out, or can they act responsibly to support a transition to renewables? Self-governance by commercial entities does not have a good track record.

SOCIETY

ABORIGINAL SETTLEMENTS

The indigenous people of Australia have survived for between 40,000 and 65,000 years and are one of the oldest cultures on the planet. In 1770 there were a quarter of a million in New South Wales but then Captain Cook arrived. By the end of the century smallpox had wiped out 70 per cent of them. One hundred years on, 90 per cent of the further generations died either from disease or through massacre.

When the Australian Parliament granted the indigenous peoples self-determination in the 1970s, together with funding, they learned to exercise it freely. This lasted until the 1990s, when the government withdrew financial support for remote settlements; investments into healthcare, education and law and order, had apparently delivered weak 'outcomes'. By 2005 the backlash was popular enough for the federal minister for Indigenous Affairs to publicly criticize small outstations as 'cultural museums'.

Government intervention has grown since 2007, with a proposal that they relocate the people to larger, 'more efficient' centres. It genuinely seems there's a human welfare crisis, particularly in respect of housing for many of the settlements. There's also the problem of alcohol-related crime, as exemplified in Tennant Creek, which suffers so badly that the Aboriginal corporations have themselves asked for tougher restrictions on pubs, clubs and bottle shops.

While the government rationale for resettlement may look good on a spreadsheet, and the strategy seem reasonable in the name of social reform, the indigenous peoples have a distinct culture. Some have profoundly different aspirations to city dwellers, and would rather be self-reliant in arid outstations than deal with the alien social pressures of urban centres.

SALMON

In 1980, there were about nine million wild salmon in the ocean, and this has dropped by two-thirds in forty years. Over the same period, because of the melting of polar ice caps, their normal feeding grounds have retracted towards the North and South Poles where cold water meets the warmer currents. In addition, the threats of hydroelectric power, pollution, overfishing, netting for other species, predators and disease have increased. Together, these are causing a huge decline in the world population of salmon, particularly in the Atlantic.

There's now a movement to reverse this through a simple, low-cost restoration programme. The strategy is to protect smolts (young salmon) where they're born. This 'semi-natural rearing' (SNR), takes advantage of the fact that salmon instinctively spawn in fresh water. By allowing them to develop healthily in a protected environment, they stand the best chance of surviving when they reach the ocean, and later breeding successfully on their return. Case studies in Cornwall and on the River Wye in the UK have shown this to work, as have variations on the theme in Scandinavia and other countries.

Curiously, the scheme has met with vigorous opposition from certain quarters. The PR machine for salmon farms blame wild fish for the infestation of sea-lice in their stocks, rather than their own bad practices, leading to the destruction of hundreds of thousands of fish. They also claim (without evidence) that ranching of fish in this way will 'dilute the gene stock' of wild salmon. Conservationists point out that migratory wild salmon have survived successfully since the Ice Age, 2.4 million years ago. The more likely cause is the quality of animal welfare on fish farms.

SHERLOCK KNOWS BEST

The sale of opium was not a crime in nineteenth-century England. Opium dens, such as those featured in the Sherlock Holmes mystery 'The Man with the Twisted Lip' were synonymous with the underworld. Yet when our hero smoked an ounce of tobacco in the name of solving the riddle, our only concern for his health was the threat posed by villains. There again, Sherlock smoked a pipe ...

More than sixty countries worldwide now demand that cigarette and hand-rolling tobacco packaging carries explicit written health warnings. In the UK, the government prescribes the layout of the display, images and specific messages. One such reads 'Smoke contains benzene, nitrosamines, formaldehyde and hydrogen cyanide'. Benzene affects the nervous system and is a known carcinogen; nitrosamines are associated with the risk of oesophageal and gastric cancer; formaldehyde is an irritant to the nose, throat and eyes (and used to preserve dead bodies); and the Nazis exploited hydrogen cyanide in their gas chambers. It is no longer a requirement to list the six hundred chemicals used in the curing process for cigarette tobacco (aka shag) and which have harmful effects when released in smoke. These additives are absent from good pipe tobacco.

Less well publicized are the chemicals in cigarette papers, which include potassium nitrate (also used to cure meat) to ensure an even burn. For the last hundred years, the bleaching agent of choice for cigarette papers has been chlorine. When burned, this releases the serious industrial pollutant dioxin, also known as the defoliant Agent Orange.

Perhaps the uncontaminated mind of Sherlock Holmes would deduce an intrigue in the continued sanction of poisonous chemicals in cigarette products?

PRIVACY ON THE SMARTPHONE

In Victorian times, there was a certain class of gent whose business was to relieve others of their wallets, watches and gems. These were the pick-pockets who infested London streets in a not-so-benign culture of 'grab-it-while-you-can-or-end-up-in-the-workhouse'. Many ended up somewhere worse.

Nowadays, no one need stoop to such low cunning to fill their boots with money. I'm not talking of the benign influence of the welfare state, nor the high moral standards of twenty-first-century business, but rather of the easy pickings available through technology.

Smartphones all have downloadable apps that supplement the standard fare distributed with ex-factory devices. This third-party software has to comply with the standards imposed by the distributor, yet that leaves plenty of room for manoeuvre.

The scam goes like this: you download a must-have app to your handset; you accept the terms and conditions with barely a glance (the app is probably free anyway) and immediately play the game, or flash the torch on or off, or whatever. Meanwhile, the app is contentedly helping itself to anything the programmers have dictated it should plunder. Even the photograph you may be taking.

Fear not, gentle reader, for the information you've given them is likely to be 'anonymized', before being shared with interested parties. After all, you accepted their offer of a free lunch ...

QUANTUM TELEPORTATION FOR BEGINNERS

Before we start, let me make this clear: this is nothing to do with time travel, or Kirk being beamed up to the Starship Enterprise. Neither can I give you any context for the science of quantum computing (which has apparently spawned some remarkable experiments), but please stick with me. Here's a fact: in 2010, scientists faithfully transmitted the quantum version of a computer 'bit', from one place to another 16 kilometres away, without the bit itself being transferred through space.

To me, this sounds like a decent short-distance telephone call, however the interesting bit (*sic*) is apparently in the application. While we can't use this transmission for communication at speeds faster than light, it is quick, tiny and the Chinese reckon on an 89 per cent success rate. A year later, scientists sent packets of light within a certain bandwidth using the same technology. From that point onward,

I cannot follow. I suspect that this will have applications other than the delivery of a lightning bolt on command, but then again, who hasn't wished to have godlike powers at some point? I'm still reeling at the miracle of day and night.

The reason for telling you all this, is neither to show off my scientific knowledge, nor to dazzle you with the latest gossip from the world of quantum mechanics. It's simply that without the unique resource of Wikipedia and the educated minds who accurately inform the articles, I doubt that modern man could make any sense of this subject, at any level.

Let's protect our valuables.

RELIEF ROADS

The planning of a road to relieve congestion in an urban area is an important decision, and likely to stir strong emotions for all those affected. When traffic clogs the heart of a town, it brings noise, fumes and hazards to those crossing it. Action needs to be taken; but which way to go? Now that computer modelling is widely available, it's possible to evaluate all the options as long as care is taken to provide rigorously researched data, and to consider the outcomes in economic, social and environmental impact. This is the 'triple bottom line' needed to determine a truly sustainable development. The environmental assessment is critically important, as natural features will never return once they're gone.

Along with roadway extensions, there are three other strategies to tackle congestion, and these are 'alternative', 'financial' and 'smart growth'. Walking, cycling, rideshares, public transit systems and teleworking come under the first category. Parking costs, toll fees and congestion charges are in the second. The third requires a lot more foresight and integration; it's a different approach to town planning. This involves mixing up housing and facilities to produce a local village node, which allows people to get what they need from where they live.

Modern research reveals that new roads often don't deliver the anticipated relief, and have the additional pain of very high capital cost. Furthermore, in the very act of construction, they effectively redefine the boundary of a town and encourage infill with property developments. Both man and nature lose.

DRIVING OFFENCES

The rules and regulations for using public highways are designed to keep people from harm, and therefore fall under the category of civil rather than criminal law. In the UK, the Highway Code provides all the definitions of correct behaviour on the roads. Most offences, such as speeding or driving without a seatbelt, carry simple fixed-penalty notices. Inconsiderate or antisocial behaviour, such as drink-driving, results in disqualification. Evidence in these situations is measurable, and decisions can therefore be made efficiently. In the case of a collision, the mistake is self-evident and the question is simply, 'Whose fault is this?'

A less binary situation is presented when one driver takes issue with another and demands compensation. This requires the plaintiff (aka 'the claimant') to establish a set of facts that justify their right to sue the defendant, together with the legal theory behind the action. The key proof points are to identify the duty of the other road user, the breach of that duty, the consequences of the breach and thus the grounds for damages. The defendant may accept guilt, or deny it and in turn mount a positive, evidence-based defence.

In some cases, the emotion of the claimant (or their fear of being found in the wrong themselves) lures them into believing they're correct to pursue a claim. If they don't convince the court of their case beyond reasonable doubt, the action will be dismissed for 'failure to state a claim'. The defendant must simply stand their ground.

◉

WHITHER POWER?

Historians attribute the long duration of the Chinese Empire to the 'men of talent and merit', the mandarins, employed in this very early example of a civil service. That tradition is carried on in some, but not all administrations, where the credentials, training and suitability of candidates are formally examined. While policies may be overseen by democratically elected representatives in central government, they're created, developed and delivered in a bureaucracy. In the 'the Mother of Parliaments' in the UK, there's a headcount of nearly half a million officials spread across numerous departments and agencies, as well as about a thousand other bodies (quangos) with a high degree of autonomy. These remote limbs of government operate outside public control and both the public and media frequently raise concerns, stating they are highly inefficient. Many of the quangos have the freedom to decide operational priorities, and thus may determine policies with little or no genuine public consultation.

At local authority level, decision-making is usually undertaken by committees of executives. More bureaucrats. In theory, they report to elected councillors, who have a legal duty of getting the best value for the public. This value is primarily economic, and not measured by social or environmental impact. As councillors are elected by the public, often with a very small turnout at the ballot box, there is no obligation on them to have the necessary skills to assess this value.

Logically, therefore, the vitality of democracy relies on us – the citizens on the street – to ensure those of genuine 'talent and merit' have authority at every level. Once an issue is drawn into the vast machinery of government, it can be very hard to influence policy.

◉

HOW YOU VOTE

A survey of thirty countries in Europe has shown that we vote more conservatively when we're in view of a church building. This suggests our surroundings affect us directly. Indeed, the word used by psychologists to refer to emotions in play on a decision is 'affect'. Our age also has its sway: as George Bernard Shaw (among others) quipped, 'If you are not a socialist by the time you're twenty-five, you have no heart. If you're not a Conservative by the time you're thirty-five, you have no head.' In wartime, older statesmen are chosen, perhaps because they're meant to be less impulsive. In peace-time, younger politicians are systematically preferred. Naturally, the media we choose to consume will broadly reflect our opinions, and therefore it's no surprise we will tend to follow their points of view in turn.

There was a time that one's social position was

an accurate barometer of how we vote. Now, in our 'information-rich' society, it's more likely to be a mix of facts filtered by our leaning, fancy and the candidate's popularity on social media.

Successful advertising is based on the premise that we the consumers s make purchasing decisions with our hearts and our loins, and not our heads. It'll therefore come as no surprise to you that we choose our leaders by age, social status and gender. We also select by attractiveness (in the case of men choosing women), approachability (vice versa) and perceived competence. Thus, the data behind our perceptions is typically gathered by trial and error and subject to our usual unconscious biases. But what of the issues, the manifestos, the cut and thrust of the House? They play their part, but a US survey discovered most people voted according to the way a candidate's face looked. The warmer the face, the more likely a Democrat.

◉

POLITICS

SPECIAL INTERESTS

The coat of arms used by Her Majesty's Government includes the text 'Honi soit qui mal y pense', which translates as 'shamed be the person who thinks evil of it.'

The parliamentary code of conduct is a substantial but readable publication. It requires Members to declare their 'special interests', both in a public register and on engaging in debates or other official proceedings. Such interests include directorships, shareholdings, services to clients ('parliamentary advice'), overseas visits, land or property, employment, sponsorships, as well as gifts and hospitality. Some commercial relationships are exempt from the register, but the code of conduct is specific that a Member must declare an interest if it may be thought an influence.

Sadly, there are occasions – even today in the venerable and revered chamber of the House – in which members 'inadvertently' forget to declare substantial payments; or are the chair of a sensitive select committee, when they have a six-figure income from vested interests; or a large number of those voting on tax reform are revealed to be either directors, or with controlling interests in companies based in offshore tax havens. If the UK is to maintain a reputation as a respected democracy, it must evidently be free of corruption. We therefore need a direct and clear process for correcting the errors of Members of Parliament. When a breach is substantiated by good evidence, they should be removed from office while the matter is promptly investigated and a judgement made.

As Juvenal said, 'Quis custodiet ipsos custodies?' or 'Who will watch the watchmen themselves?'

GRANTS

The attraction of 'free' money given out by aid agencies, government departments and local authorities is obvious, but there are hidden traps that cause damage to both the intended recipients and the system itself.

The motive for granting aid aspires to one of three categories: economic investment, political influence and simple goodwill to meet a need. Investment is the simplest to understand, as it replaces the need for conventional ways of fund-raising, such as equity sharing or loans, with a cheaper option. There are usually clear regulations associated with such gifts. Unearned income discourages recipients from exploring traditional sources of funds, induces the lucky ones to wait for the next dollop of cash, and tends to prop up unsustainable businesses. Political influence includes areas which need support to meet strategic goals, such as long-term, large-scale scientific research. Unfortunately, it also includes 'buying' job creation which, by definition, is unsustainable. Goodwill gestures, such as reaching out to a failed region, are perhaps the most contentious. The benefits may be entirely desirable on humanitarian grounds, but the hazards are acute. The concerns include the transparency of agents distributing the funds, delays to economic reform and the actual use of the money for the intended aim. In the case of Uganda from the 1990s onward, the influx of grants caused an acceleration in military spending.

In 2008, we all saw what happens when banks filter cash through a large number of opaque organizations, and so too with the distribution of grants to unaccountable recipients. Smart money now measures the things that matter through a calculation of the 'social return on investment'. Not before time.

◉

CHILD SLAVERY

There are 27 million slaves worldwide and, for obvious reasons, there are few further demographics about them. Over 300,000 children are working in dangerous conditions on cocoa farms on the west coast of Africa, half of them under fourteen and at least 6,000 'unpaid with no family ties'. Cameroon, for instance, is one of these cocoa-producing areas. There is slavery in the country's north, which is both a source, transit route and destination for child trafficking. Victims end up in Scandinavia, Europe and even the USA.

Although Cameroon has one of the best primary commodity economies in sub-Saharan Africa (it has both oil and good agricultural conditions) it's afflicted by poverty, uneven government, a lack of public services and no child protection laws. In theory, education is compulsory to age fourteen (the minimum age of legal employment), but 60 per cent don't even complete primary school.

There is abundant evidence that a society prospers when girls are well educated, as they then ensure their daughters and sons are similarly schooled. In Cameroon, many girls become child brides. A report in 2000 found that 11 per cent of kids drop out of primary school. They do over four hours of labour per day as domestic help, while the rest work in agriculture, mining, street vending, sweatshops and prostitution.

Perhaps the most bitter stories are from children whose family has handed them over to those promising 'education and a better life in the city'. While Fair Trade labelling on a bar of chocolate may assure us of a cocoa grower's farming standards, it does not protect children from exploitation.

INDIAN HEGEMONY

Hegemony is the dominance of one group over another, to the degree that the subordinates perform to satisfy the leader's interests, usually to the detriment of their own. Such a state could be said of Tibet following the Chinese invasion in 1950, although to this day there remains resistance in the country, in western China and internationally. It certainly existed in British colonial rule of the Indian subcontinent, which went far beyond bureaucracy into many aspects of culture, language and behaviour.

We now have the rapid growth of India herself, raising disputes over land ownership, water use, environmental damage and civil rights with her neighbours in Pakistan, Bangladesh and Nepal. While India's outward political position is that of a liberal democracy, her behaviour regarding the Tipaimukh Dam on the Bangladesh border has been heavy-handed. Her proposal violates five UN rulings and has been described as a 'geo-tectonic blunder', as the barrage is sited about two hundred and forty kilometres from an earthquake fault line on the Myanmar border. Foreign ministers on both sides have agreed a way forward, but geologists and local citizens appear to be far from convinced. There are similar tensions with Pakistan concerning a water-sharing agreement, as well as the long-standing territorial conflict over the former princely state of Jammu and Kashmir.

While India's star is in the ascendant as a member of the Indo-Pacific superpower trading bloc of Australia, Vietnam, Japan, Thailand and South Korea, it would be wise to balance its might with compassion, and to show leadership based on friendship and dignity. As Gandhi said, 'I suppose leadership at one time meant muscles; but today it means getting along with people.'

STILL WATERS RUN DEEP

The saying 'still waters run deep' suggests a placid exterior covering a profound or subtle character, but in ancient times it meant the concealment of dangerous qualities. Practical knowledge of rivers will confirm fast-moving smooth water tells of depth, and a noisy babbling tells of shallows.

Far out in the ocean one's unlikely to find much still water, but in the Mariana Trench – formed by two vast diverging tectonic plates of the Pacific – there's nearly seven miles' distance from the surface to the seabed. It's also the narrowest point between the solid surface of Earth's crust and the outer molten core, about three thousand kilometres straight down.

Between 1954 and 1993 the USSR, UK, Switzerland, USA, Belgium, France, the Netherlands, Japan, Sweden, Russia, New Zealand, Germany, Italy and South Korea all used ocean-disposal of nuclear waste. Advocates recommended the use of the Mariana Trench in the hope that the continuous movement of the two vast plates would fold radioactive substances into the earth's crust. They estimated the initial radioactivity at the time of the dump to be 85.1 × 1015 becquerels. This is less than 1 per cent of the total release from either Chernobyl (1986) or Fukushima Daiichi (2011), but pollution from these incidents was airborne and therefore more easily dissipated.

Fortunately for us, international law banned the ocean-dumping of nuclear waste in 1994, before countries put their novel scheme into action. The proponents appear to have ignored the fact that the Mariana Trench is also a site of mega-thrust earthquakes, with highly unpredictable results.

Still waters run deep, even in the ocean.

TRIDENT

In 1980 the UK bought into the US Trident programme, for submarine-launched missiles with nuclear warheads, at an estimated cost of £5 billion. At the time, a nuclear deterrent was seen as desirable; there had been growing tension between the Warsaw Pact countries, including Soviet Russia and the West. With hindsight we view this tension – a second Cold War – as a symptom of the disintegration of the communist bloc. The weapons were 'de-targeted' in 1994, but it left a question: what to do with nuclear arms now that the strategic risk (an attack from Russia) had vanished? The answer came back that it was useful to have a nuclear threat in order to menace others as a form of political coercion, the idea being that a 'small' attack wouldn't invite a nuclear exchange. It was further proposed that conventional warheads might be used on existing missiles, and thus reach from the west coast of Scotland (where the UK submarines are based) to Yakutsk in the far eastern Russian territories, seven thousand miles away. As radar cannot distinguish between conventional and nuclear warheads, the matter was dropped.

Setting aside the appalling global environmental damage of using atomic weapons, the use of such devices directly violates the universal law that distinguishes combatants from civilians. While the UK may have committed to the lease of a very expensive system from the US, Britain must now consider whether the value of projecting themselves as a 'great power' is worth the attendant moral corrosion and expenditure. Now, let's discuss the environmental cost ...

◉

MOX

Plutonium is created from the use of uranium in nuclear reactors, and has been produced by the UK's Sellafield plant since it was commissioned in 1956. The site now holds over 112 tonnes, the largest stockpile of plutonium in the world. The UK government decided to accumulate the material, as a result of the prediction that uranium would run out. Wrong. This mistake was compounded by the assumption that experimental fast breeder reactors (FBR) would become viable, and that there would be a ready market for reprocessed plutonium. Wrong again. The FBR programme was cancelled in the 1990s, as the reactors were clearly shown to be neither safe nor cost-effective. The government then offered to reprocess the nuclear waste of other countries – particularly Germany and Japan – to generate revenue. The idea was that these countries would then accept it for re-use. Wrong, yet again. About one quarter of the material held at Sellafield comes from abroad, and no one seems to want it back.

In 1993 the government gave approval for the building of a mixed oxide (Mox) plant at Sellafield. This nuclear fuel is based on reprocessed plutonium used in thermal reactors with normal water, such as Fukushima Daiichi. By 2006 the Mox plant was shown to be operating with six thousand minor equipment failures in the space of two months, yet was deemed 'too expensive to fail'. However, when a tsunami engulfed Fukushima in 2011, and Japan cancelled a reprocessing contract, it forced the closure of the Mox plant at an estimated cost of £1.4 billion.

Sellafield remains Europe's largest nuclear site.

◉

THE COST OF CAPITAL

In Marxist terms, capital is what you use to buy something, to sell it on at a profit. In financial markets, the cost of capital is an assessment of how much it costs to commit assets to a project by comparing it to an alternative investment. Although these are cornerstones of a capitalist society, there is more than one type of asset and there are therefore a variety of ways to consider value.

In 1890, Alex de Tocqueville wrote of the American democratic system that it 'encouraged many meetings, which led to much transparency, participation, and therefore engagement in a healthy society'. This is an example of social capital as open engagement essential to good governance and strong communities. It's impossible to measure this in economic terms, but dividends from this include high levels of trust and freedom of choice, enjoyed by both individuals and groups. This cultural and spiritual diversity may seem disorganized – humans are not simple units behaving in an orderly, financially efficient way – but it is highly valuable for civilization.

There is also natural capital inherent in the environment that supports life. We all neglect it at our peril. Researchers tried to evaluate the seventeen major ecosystems that support the earth's biosphere, and estimated they deliver services worth $33 trillion per annum. That may have been their 'cost of capital' at that moment in time, but what would we do without them? What's the alternative?

The Kingdom of Bhutan attempts to resolve this by emphasizing the factors of sustainable development, cultural values, natural environment and good governance. They reckon that we need to serve the roots of happiness, rather than money for its own sake.

◉

LA CLASSE STERILE

At the age of just twenty-nine, Adam Smith (1723–1790) became head of moral philosophy at Glasgow University. He later referred to the thirteen years he spent there as, 'by far the happiest and most honourable period [of my life]'. Halfway through this tenure, a collection of his lectures was published as *The Theory of Moral Sentiments*, which states that empathy between people is the key to ethical conduct. That is, observation of others and sympathy with them makes one more aware of oneself and of a moral code. This is from the same man who, money-makers claim, gives them authority to practise modern capitalism. Perhaps this is not the whole truth.

Smith was part of the Scottish Enlightenment, which demanded solid reasoning as the basis behind decisions, and declared that no authority was above this. His later work, which includes the famous

Wealth of Nations, was greatly influenced by contact with the Physiocrats, a group of French economists. They believed that agriculture and the development of land was the sole measure of national wealth. Although this strand of thought became particularly popular as a rebuke to *la classe sterile* of unproductive aristocrats, it also chimed with Smith's conclusions. He recognized that when natural human self-interest seeks the most reward from farming or other useful production, and competitive market forces are also present, then everyone benefits. He called this 'the invisible hand' that causes a community to regulate itself.

Many financial and other global services don't assist with the production of goods, and therefore fail to meet this criterion.

AFTERWORD

Your opinion of ***espresso***, given as a review on Amazon, is highly valuable to me. If it's positive, it will encourage me to write more and help others to identify a book worth reading. If it's negative, then I'll learn and correct myself! Either way, I will read and appreciate your review.

Review page on Amazon

Bonus

Please be sure to sign up to the monthly newsletter at my website and I'll keep you posted on new releases.

You'll also receive the free ***espresso*** sampler of a further fifteen original pieces.

ALSO BY ORLANDO KIMBER

Available now

'...modern, interesting and fun...' ***The Independent***

Amazon reader reviews include:

'a book about people and people are important'

'excellent pacy, exciting, easy-to-read novel meticulously researched, intriguing and only too believable'

'A gripping, page-turning, contemporary political eco-thriller.'

ABOUT ORLANDO

Orlando grew up in London, became a musician playing guitar and percussion, and worked as a producer and composer for tv and film.

He then moved into international broadcasting, and led campaigns including the Digital Revolution of the BBC and the launch of the internet in Europe. Subsequently, he lived and worked in the Middle East, where he ran a consultancy.

His wife fell seriously ill in 2012, and together they moved to Cornwall, where she has family roots. Orlando began writing and campaigning for both ethical governance and for protection of the natural environment.

He produces popular non-fiction and fiction, and hosts the podcast *Orlando Kimber's Good Company* which focuses on ethics in business.

Thank you to Boo for your constant inspiration,
to my family and friends for their support,
and to all the readers in sixty-four countries worldwide.
Cover design by Modern Activity

First e-print: November 2021

espresso is a publication from
The Arthur & Moose Publishing Company

Printed in Great Britain
by Amazon

77089383R00066